The Illustrated Rules of
BASKETBALL

By Frank Bennett
Illustrated by Paul Zuehlke

Ideals Children's Books • Nashville, Tennessee

For Jan, Franklin, Lee, and Laura.
Thanks for your love and support.
                    —F.B.

For my son, Adam.
                    —P.Z.

Special thanks to George, Matt, Courtney, and Adam for
modeling for the pictures in this book.

Published by Ideals Children's Books
An imprint of Hambleton-Hill Publishing, Inc.
Nashville, Tennessee 37218

Printed and bound in the United States of America

Library of Congress Cataloging-in-Publication Data
Bennett, Frank, 1951–
    The illustrated rules of basketball / by Frank Bennett ; illustrated by Paul Zuehlke
      p.   cm.
    ISBN 1-57102-021-7
    1. Basketball—Rules—Juvenile literature. [1. Basketball—Rules.] I. Zuehlke, Paul,
    ill. II. Title.
    GV885.45.B46   1994
    796.323'02'022—dc20   94-1909
                                       CIP
                                        AC

Reviewed and endorsed by Junior Pro, Inc.

Table of Contents

Note to Parents:

This book offers an excellent way to capture and hold the interest of young basketball players, to inform them of important points of the game, and to facilitate discussion of the game by players and their parents.

The rules in this book were written by an experienced basketball coach drawing from his own experience, from basketball tradition, and from rules that are accepted worldwide and used in various forms by respected organizations such as Junior Pro, Inc., the Amateur Athletic Union, the National Federation of State High School Associations, and the NCAA.

These pages present the rules in simplified form so that they can be easily understood by young players. Information was selected on the basis of what would be of most interest to young players and parents and most suitable for discussion.

The Game of Basketball

The game of basketball is one of the few major sports that had its beginnings in the United States. It was invented in 1891 by Dr. James A. Naismith, who wanted to develop a sport that could be played inside during the cold winter months. The first basketball hoop was a peach basket. The players used a ladder to get the ball after a basket was made.

Today basketball is a fast-paced and exciting game that is played by boys and girls and men and women of all ages. A team of five players tries to shoot the ball into a basket while another team of five tries to stop them. Basketball requires a lot of teamwork and passing in order to get good shots. The team with the most points at the end of the game wins.

Baskctball has become more and more popular and many games can be seen on TV. Professional stars such as Larry Bird, Magic Johnson, and Michael Jordan have helped increase the popularity of the game. In 1992, a "Dream Team" made of the best professional and college players played in the Olympics and brought the game a lot of attention.

If you are interested in basketball, the players, and the history of the game, you may want to visit the Basketball Hall of Fame in Springfield, Massachusetts, where the game was invented.

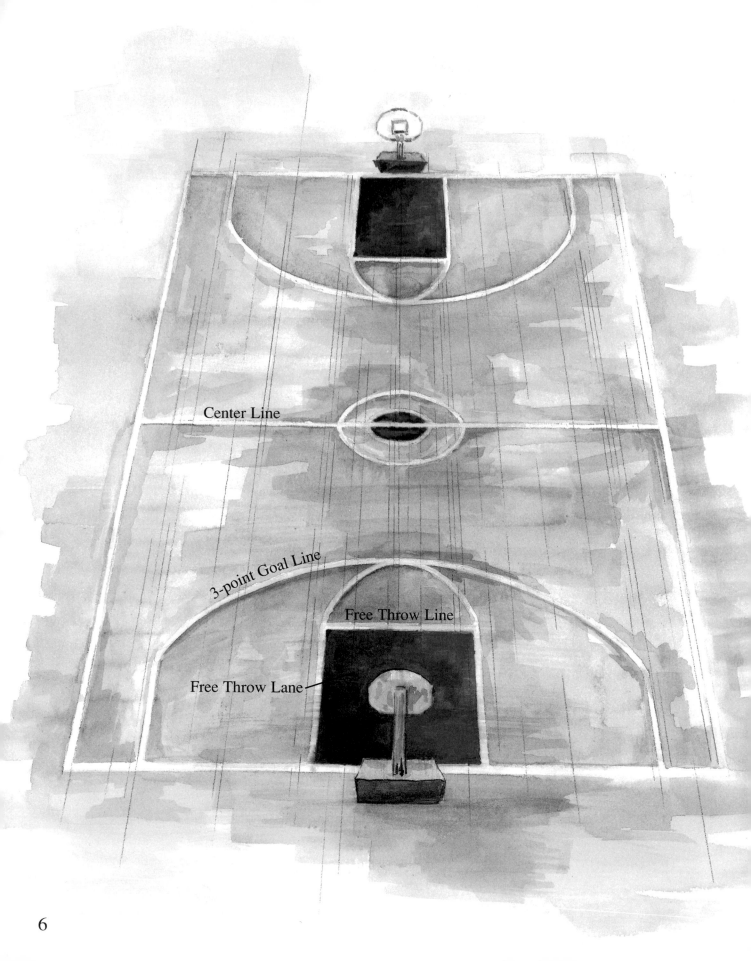

Center Line

3-point Goal Line

Free Throw Line

Free Throw Lane

The Rules of the Game

Rule 1: The Court

The basketball court is in the shape of a rectangle. The size of the court may be different at different levels of competition.

A **center line** separates the floor into a front court and a backcourt for the team that has the ball.

The **3-point goal line** is a half-circle around the basket. Any goals made from behind this line count for 3 points.

The **free throw line** is 15 feet from the backboard. The free throw lane is 12 feet wide.

Rule 2: The Basket

The basket is a metal ring that is 18 inches across with a net hanging from the ring. The basketball goal is usually 10 feet high, although youth leagues may use shorter goals (for example, Junior Pro Training and Junior Varsity leagues use 9-foot goals).

Rule 3: The Ball

The ball is a shade of orange or a natural color. It is pebbled and is divided into panels by black rubber ribs. The circumference (the distance around the outside) of the ball is generally $29\frac{1}{2}$ to 30 inches for boys and $28\frac{1}{2}$ to 29 inches for girls. Youth leagues sponsored by the Amateur Athletic Union, YMCA-sponsored youth leagues, and Junior Pro Basketball teams sometimes use a smaller ball.

Rule 4: The Officials

There are either two or three officials for a basketball game—a **referee** and one or two **umpires**. Their job is to enforce the rules of the game. They are in charge as soon as they come onto the floor. The officials use a whistle to stop the game when a foul or violation occurs or when a ball or player is out-of-bounds.

Rule 5: The Players

A team generally has one captain. Only five players on a team may be on the floor at one time. Substitutes may replace players in the game.

A substitute who is about to enter the game must first report to the scorer and give his or her number and the number of the player who is being replaced. A substitute may not enter the game until the ball is dead and the clock is stopped. The official must beckon the substitute to enter the game.

Rule 6: Game Time

Professional basketball teams usually play four twelve-minute quarters with one-minute breaks after the first and third quarters and with a fifteen-minute halftime between the second and third quarters. College teams play two twenty-minute halves with a fifteen-minute break between halves. Playing time for teams of high school age is four eight-minute quarters with one-minute breaks after the first and third quarters and with a ten-minute halftime. Youth leagues such as Junior Pro and school games using only students below the ninth grade play six-minute quarters.

Extra periods, or **overtimes**, are played when the score is tied at the end of the fourth quarter or at the end of an overtime period. The length of an overtime period is three minutes.

Rule 7: Scoring

A **goal** is scored when a live ball enters the basket from above and remains in the basket or passes through the net. A ball going through the basket from below is a violation and does not count.

A goal scored from behind the 3-point goal line counts for 3 points.

A free throw counts for 1 point.

All other goals count for 2 points.

3-point Goal

Free Throw

13

Jump Ball

Rule 8: Starting the Game

A **jump ball** is used to put the ball in play at the beginning of a game or an overtime period. The referee tosses the ball up between two opponents at the center circle. Each of these players tries to tap the ball to a teammate.

Rule 9:
Alternating Possession

Alternating possession is the rule for putting the ball back in play when there is a held ball or when two players on opposing teams cause the ball to go out-of-bounds at the same time. Alternating possession means that the teams take turns in getting possession of the ball.

The method used to keep track of which team is to get the ball next may be an arrow that lights up, an arrow-shaped piece of wood that is turned back and forth by hand, or it may be as simple as making a mark in a score book.

A **held ball** is when two or more opponents have their hands grasping the ball so that neither one can control it without being too rough.

Held Ball

Alternating Possession Arrow

Rule 10: Fouls

A **personal foul** is a **contact foul**. This happens when a player makes contact with an opponent in a way that is against the rules. A player is not allowed to hold, push, charge, trip, or try to stop a player on the other team by holding out an arm, shoulder, hip, or knee. A **technical foul** is one of three different kinds of fouls. It can be a noncontact foul by a player, a contact foul made when the ball is dead, or a foul by a nonplayer such as a coach or manager.

When an official calls a foul, the ball is awarded out-of-bounds to the other team, or it may be awarded to the other team for a free throw.

A player who is charged with five fouls can no longer play in the game.

Personal Foul

Rule 11: Free Throw

A **free throw** is a chance to score 1 point without being guarded by members of the opposing team. The free throw shooter stands in the foul circle behind the foul line. Players from the other team stand in the lane spaces next to the basketball goal. Teammates of the free throw shooter will alternate with opponents for the remaining positions on the lane.

A player is awarded two free throws if he or she is fouled while shooting.

When a player who is not shooting the ball is fouled, the ball is awarded out-of-bounds to his or her team—unless the team has already been fouled seven times in a half. Beginning on this seventh foul, a team is awarded a **bonus** or **one and one** free throw. This means that if the shooter makes the first free throw, he or she is awarded a second free throw. If the first shot is missed, the ball is live and the game simply continues.

17

Passing

Dribbling

Dribbling

Guarding

Rule 12: Movement with the Ball

A player may not run or walk while holding the ball. This is called **traveling** and is a violation. A player may move one foot while holding the ball, but the other foot, called the **pivot foot**, must stay in one place. A player may jump off the pivot foot to shoot or pass, but must let go of the ball before returning to the floor.

A player may move with the ball by dribbling. To **dribble** means to push or tap the ball to the floor one time or several times. The ball must be dribbled using one hand at a time. A player must release the ball to dribble before moving his or her pivot foot.

A player may **pass** the ball through the air or by bouncing it off the floor to a teammate.

Kicking the ball is making contact with the ball with the knee, lower leg, or foot. When this is done on purpose, it is a violation.

Rule 13: Defense— Guarding the Opponent

To **guard** means to place the body in the path of a player on the other team. This is not against the rules. Every player has the right to any spot on the floor if he or she gets there first without illegally contacting an opponent. (Extending an arm, shoulder, hip, or leg into an opponent is illegally contacting the opponent.)

Rule 14: Out-of-Bounds

A player is out-of-bounds when he or she touches the floor or any object other than another player on or outside the boundary lines.

The ball is out-of-bounds when it touches any object, including a player, that is on or outside the boundary lines. The ball is also out-of-bounds if it touches the back of the backboard or the backboard's supports or the ceiling or the overhead equipment or supports.

When a player causes the ball to go out-of-bounds, the ball is awarded to the other team. The ball is then thrown inbounds with a **throw-in** (see Rule 15).

When two players on opposing teams cause the ball to go out-of-bounds at the same time, the ball shall be awarded to the team with the alternating possession arrow pointing in their direction (see Rule 9).

Throw-in

Rule 15: Throw-in

The ball is put into play with a **throw-in** after a basket is scored, after a violation or foul, or after the ball goes out-of-bounds.

When throwing the ball inbounds, the player must release the ball within five seconds of receiving the ball from the referee.

After a violation or a foul, or after the ball goes out-of-bounds, the player throwing in the ball must stand on the spot chosen by the referee. After a field goal or a free throw is made, the player may move along the baseline to make the inbounds pass.

Rule 16: Three Seconds in the Free Throw Lane

An offensive player may not remain in the free throw lane for longer than three seconds while his or her team has the ball in the front court.

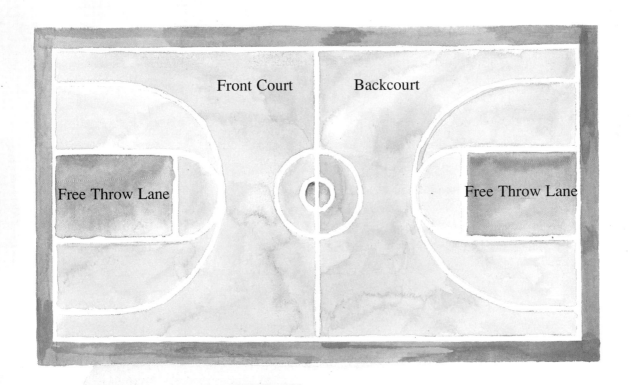

Rule 17: Front Court and Backcourt

The half of the court which contains the basket for which a team is shooting is the front court for that team, while the half of the court with the basket a team is defending is that team's backcourt. A team must advance the ball from the backcourt to the front court within ten seconds of possession of the ball. If a team has the ball in the front court, it may not return with the ball into the backcourt. This is called an **over-and-back violation**.

The Players

Each team has five players on the floor at the same time. In the early days of basketball, some players had to stay in certain areas of the court during the game. Today all five players are free to move to any area of the court and to perform any of the skills of the game.

There are two systems that designate the positions in basketball. In one system there are two guards, two forwards, and a center. This may be called the **two guard system**.

In the other system, there is a point guard, two wings, and two posts. This may be called the **point guard system**.

Some coaches prefer one system, while other coaches prefer the other. The point guard system has been used more often in recent years.

Forward

Guard

Center

Forward

Guard

The Two Guard System

The two guard system has been used for many years. Both of the guards in this system share dribbling and ball handling responsibility.

The **guards** are often smaller, quicker players who handle the ball well and dribble the ball up the floor.

The two **forwards** mostly handle the ball in the front court and usually play facing the basket.

The **center** is usually a taller player who jumps for his or her team at the jump ball that starts the game. He or she is the **post player**. A post player plays close to the basket with his or her back to the basket.

Post

Post

Wing

Wing

Point

The Point Guard System

In the point guard system, the **point guard** is responsible for most of the dribbling and ball handling. Many coaches like to have their best ball handler in this position.

The point guard is the primary dribbler and ball handler and is responsible for moving the ball up the floor and starting the team's offense.

The two **wings** usually play in the front court near the sides of the basket. Most of the time they play facing the basket. They may shoot the ball or pass it closer to the basket to a post player.

A post player usually plays at the **low post** with his or her back to the basket or at the **high post** in the foul circle area. While the two guard system has only one post player—the center—the point guard system has two post players. They may both play low post, or one may play low post and the other high post.

Important Signals of the Game

Start clock

Stop clock for jump/held ball

Stop clock

Stop clock for foul

Illegal dribble

Intentional foul

3-point field goal:
successful

Traveling

3-point field goal:
attempt

Technical foul

Sportsmanship in the Game of Basketball

One of the best things about playing basketball is that there are many important things you can learn. Teamwork and sportsmanship are two of these things.

Sportsmanship means that you play by the rules and respect the other players, the referees, and the coaches. Even though you are trying your best to beat the other team, you should not hold your opponent's jersey, swing your elbows, or do other things that are unfair. Respecting the referee is also important, even when you feel that he or she has made a mistake. Accepting the referee's decisions is just a part of the game.

Teamwork means that everyone works together for the good of the team. Nobody likes to play with a "ball hog" who never passes the ball to anyone else. It is more fun to pass the ball and work together to score points.

Some professional players do things that are not examples of good sportsmanship. If you watch a player you really like, try to copy the good things that he or she does. Watch players who show good sportsmanship and who are good team players, and try to be like them.

Summary of the Rules of Basketball

Rule 1: The Court

The basketball court is in the shape of a rectangle and has marked lines and areas that include a center line, a 3-point goal line, a free throw line, and a free throw lane.

Rule 2: The Basket

The basket is a metal ring 18 inches across with a net below. It is usually 10 feet high, but may be shorter in youth leagues.

Rule 3: The Ball

The ball is orange or a natural color, is 29½ to 30 inches for boys and 28½ to 29 inches for girls. It may be smaller in some youth leagues.

Rule 4: The Officials

There are either two or three officials for a basketball game—a referee and one or two umpires. Their job is to enforce the rules.

Rule 5: The Players

Only five players on a team may be on the floor at one time.

Rule 6: Game Time

Basketball games are played in quarters with breaks after the first and third quarters and a longer break between halves.

Rule 7: Scoring

A goal scored from behind the 3-point goal line counts 3 points. A free throw counts 1 point. All other goals count 2 points.

Rule 8: Starting the Game

A jump ball is the method used to put the ball in play at the beginning of a game or an overtime period.

Rule 9: Alternating Possession

Alternating possession is the rule for putting the ball back in play when there is a held ball or when two opposing players simultaneously cause the ball to go out-of-bounds.

Rule 10: Fouls

A personal foul means that a player has made illegal contact with an opponent. A technical foul is a noncontact foul, a contact foul made while the ball is dead, or a foul by a nonplayer. When an official calls a foul, the ball is awarded out-of-bounds to the other team, or it may be awarded to the other team for a free throw.

Rule 11: Free Throw

A free throw is a chance to score 1 point without being guarded by opponents.

Rule 12: Movement with the Ball

A player may move with the ball by dribbling, may pass the ball through the air, or may bounce it off the floor to a teammate.

Rule 13: Defense—Guarding the Opponent

To guard means to place the body in the path of a player on the other team.

Rule 14: Out-of-Bounds

A player and/or the ball may be out-of-bounds. When a player causes the ball to go out-of-bounds, the ball is awarded to the other team.

Rule 15: Throw-in

The ball is put into play with a throw-in after a basket is scored, after a violation or foul, or after the ball goes out-of-bounds.

Rule 16: Three Seconds in the Free Throw Lane

An offensive player may not remain in the free throw lane for longer than three seconds while his or her team has the ball in the front court.

Rule 17: Front court and Backcourt

A team must advance the ball from the backcourt to the front court within ten seconds of possession of the ball.

Vocabulary of the Game

backcourt: the half of the court containing the basket that a team is defending

center: the player who jumps for his or her team at the jump ball that begins the game

double dribble: a violation in which a player dribbles with two hands or dribbles, catches the ball, and then dribbles again

forward: a player who plays in the front court, usually facing the basket

front court: the half of the court containing the basket for which a team is shooting is the front court for that team

guard: to place the body in the path of a player on the opposing team; also, a player who plays in the backcourt

high post: the area around the foul circle

live ball: a ball that is being played during actual game time and is not out-of-bounds

low post: the area close to the basket

overtime: a three-minute-long extra period which is played when the score is tied at the end of the fourth quarter or at the end of an overtime period

personal foul: occurs when a player makes contact with an opponent in a way that is against the rules, such as holding, pushing, or tripping; also called a contact foul

pivot: to step once or more than once with the same foot (the pivot foot remains in the same spot while the other foot is stepping)

point guard: the primary ball handler who moves the ball up the floor to start the team's offense

technical foul: a violation which may either be a noncontact foul by a player, a contact foul made when the ball is dead, or a foul by a nonplayer such as a coach or a manager

traveling: a violation in which a player walks or runs while holding the ball

wing: one of the players who plays in the front court on the sides of the basket